Alexander Peskanov's

THE RUSSIAN TECHNICAL REGIMEN

FOR THE PIANO

(Series of Six Books)

Exercise Volume IV

ARPEGGIOS AND BLOCK CHORDS

Technical Editor - Lynn Radcliffe

W.M. Co. 11616E

To
My Beloved Teachers in Russia,
ROSALIA MOLODIETZKAYA and her son, EMIL

IN GRATEFUL REMEMBRANCE

W.M. Co. 11616E

FOREWORD

This exercise volume is part of a series of books entitled *The Russian Technical Regimen for the Piano*. It consists of the INTRODUCTION AND GUIDE to the regimen and five exercise volumes. The Russian Technical Regimen encompasses all the technical requirements which have been in use in Russian and Soviet music schools and conservatories for more than a century.

This exercise volume presents eleven arpeggios and eleven block chords in the Russian harmonic pattern, starting from all twelve notes. The eleven arpeggios starting from C are shown in the Russian pattern exactly as it is required in the technique examinations in the Russian music schools. They serve as an example for the transpositions of the same harmonic patterns of eleven chords starting from other notes. Eventually, all arpeggios should be practiced in the Russian pattern. It is important to observe all the accents as they are indicated in the example while playing the arpeggios in the Russian pattern starting from other notes. Arpeggios allow the hands to achieve maximum flexibility and mobility at the keyboard. To become fully aware of the pattern of the eleven chords and how to play them as arpeggios, one should study Part Three (Chords) of the INTRO-DUCTION AND GUIDE to the Regimen. Instructions on performing arpeggios appears in Chapter X.

The instructions for the block chords also appear in Part Three, Chapter XI of the Guide. The first series---the eleven block chords in the Russian harmonic pattern starting from C---is presented here in the exact form (two octaves up and down in parallel motion) as is required in Russia. The transpositions of the same harmonic pattern of eleven chords starting from other notes should eventually be practiced in two octaves, up and down, in the same manner as the series starting from C. These block chord exercises will improve the stretch between fingers and serve as the best vehicle for converting weight into sound.

In all phases of *The Russian Technical Regimen for the Piano* accents must always be the foundation for the rhythm and points of relaxation. The benefits of the Regimen can accrue only if it is practiced in the proper manner with full realization of the Guide Book instructions.

Alexander Peskanov

Supplementary materials and additional teaching aids include:

Introduction and Guide ("Guide Book")

Exercise Volume I, Scales in Single Notes

Exercise Volume II, Broken Chords

Exercise Volume III, Russian Broken Chords

Exercise Volume IV, Arpeggios and Block Chords

Exercise Volume V, Scales in Double Notes: Thirds, Sixths, Octaves

Instructional Videos, "In Search of Sound"
      Produced by Classical Video Concepts, Inc.

Piano Olympics Kit, Manual and Demonstration Video
      Produced by CVC, Inc.

Piano Video Exchange, Presented by the Baldwin Piano
      and Organ Co. and CVC, Inc.

Eleven Arpeggios Starting from C*

*Presented in Russian Harmonic Pattern; see *Introduction and Guide Book,* Part Three, Chapters VI, VII and X.

W.M. Co. 11616-E

4) A Minor 6

5) F Major $\frac{6}{4}$

6) F Minor $\frac{6}{4}$

7) vii dim. 7th in D♭ Major*

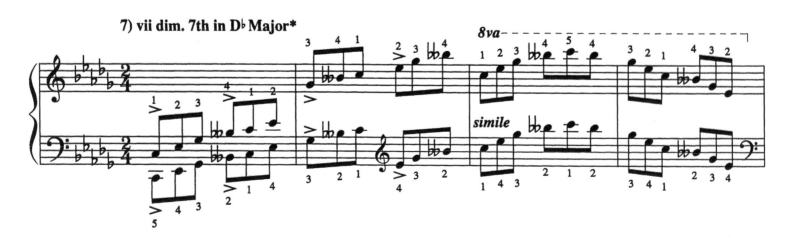

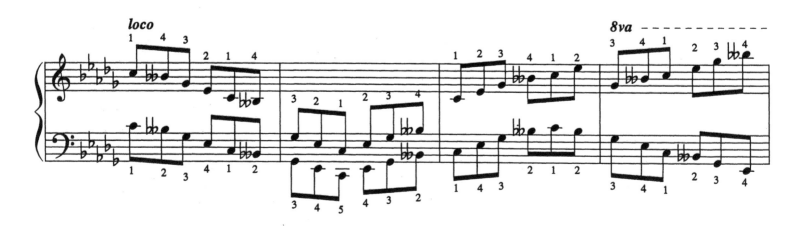

*Chords nos. 7-11 are played in triplets, accenting down beats.

8) V7 in F Major

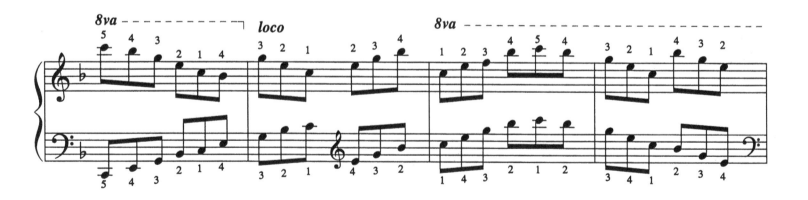

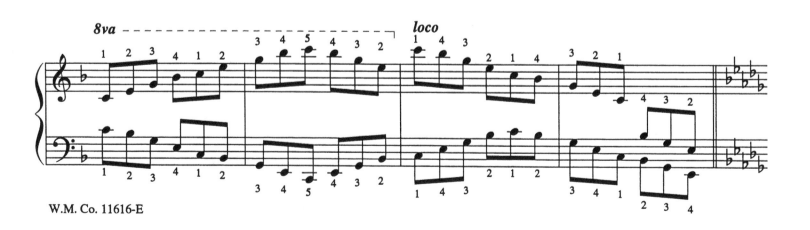

9) V $\frac{6}{5}$ in D♭ Major

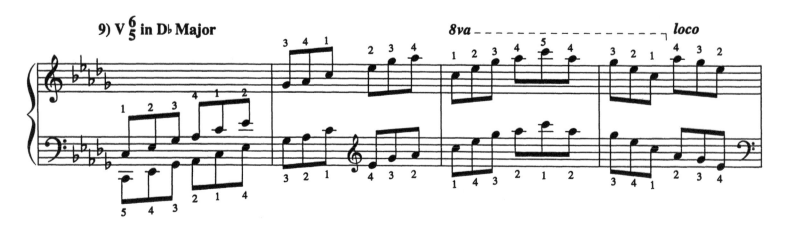

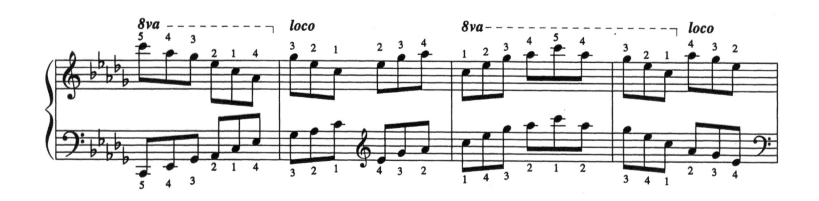

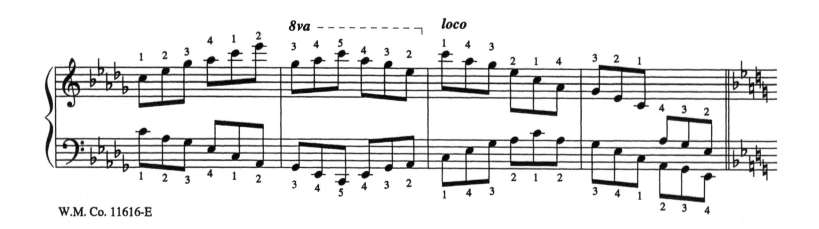

W.M. Co. 11616-E

10) V $\frac{4}{3}$ in B♭ Major

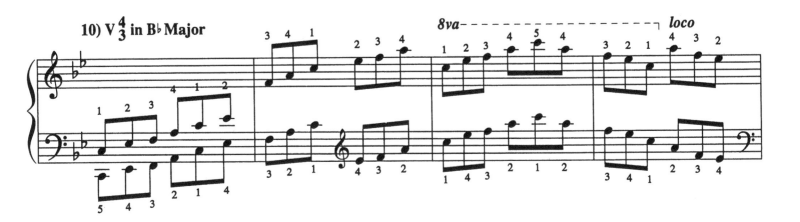

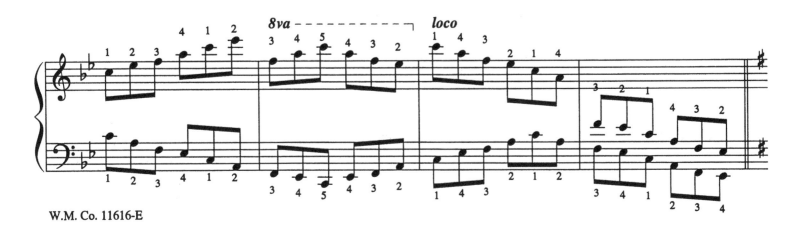

W.M. Co. 11616-E

11) V $\frac{4}{2}$ in G Major

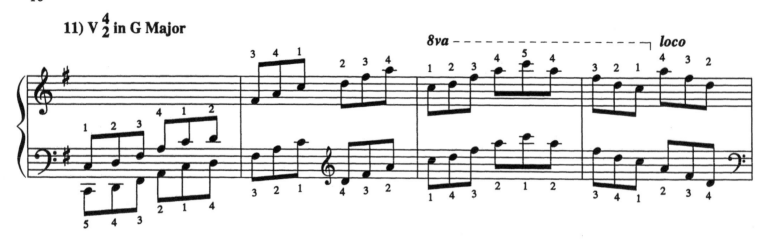

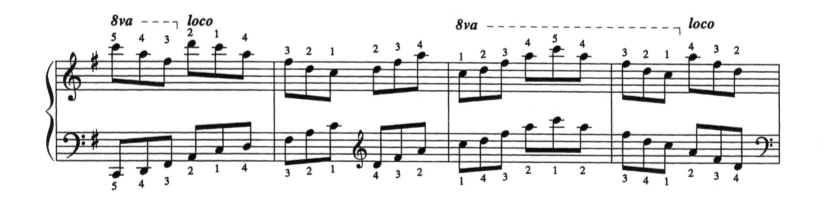

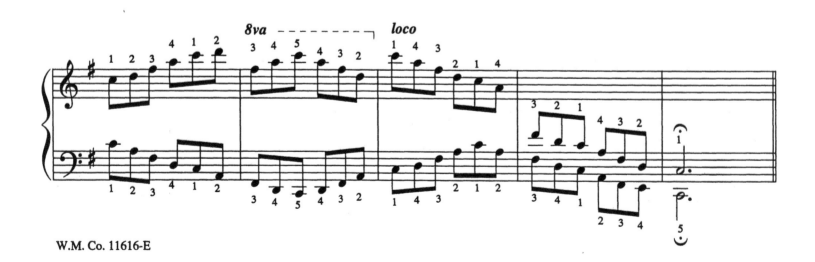

Eleven Arpeggios Starting from D♭/C♯*

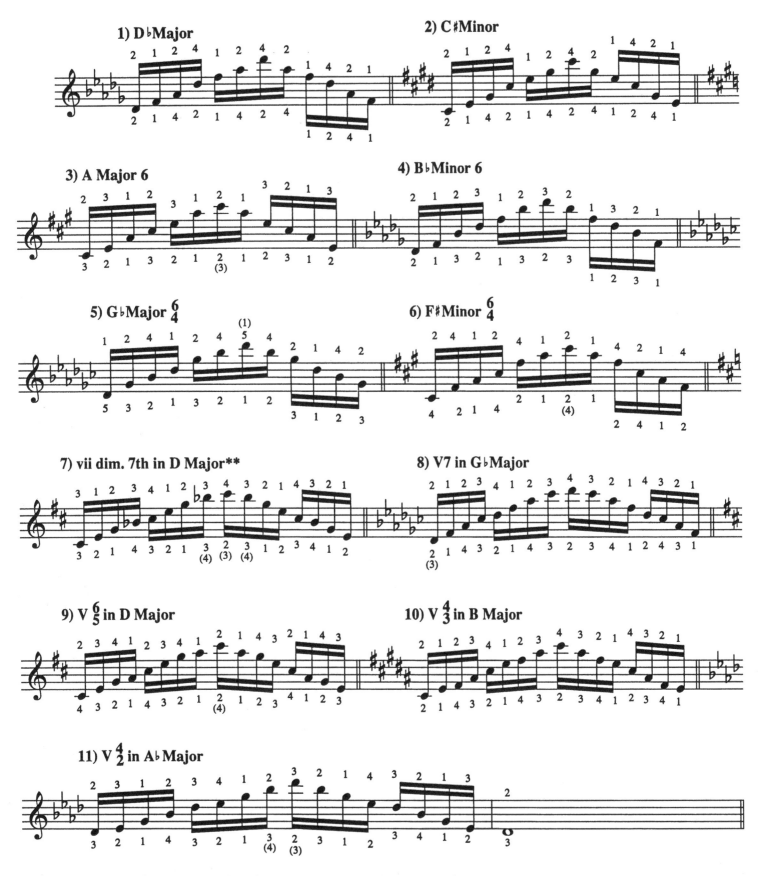

*The eleven arpeggios presented here in two octaves, parallel motion, should ultimately be played in the Russian pattern, starting from any note. See "Eleven Arpeggios Starting from C", pages 4-10.

**When playing the seventh chord arpeggios in the Russian pattern, change the meter to 6/8, accenting in "threes". See Example, pages 6-10.

W.M. Co. 11616-E

Eleven Arpeggios Starting from D

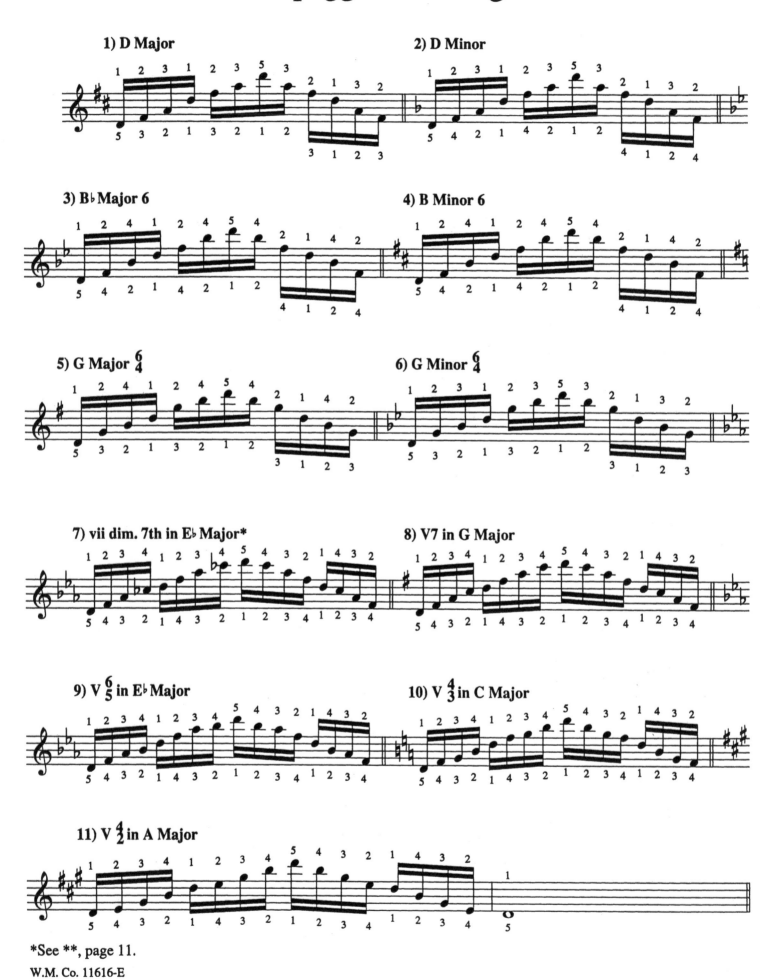

Eleven Arpeggios Starting from E♭/D♯

Eleven Arpeggios Starting from E

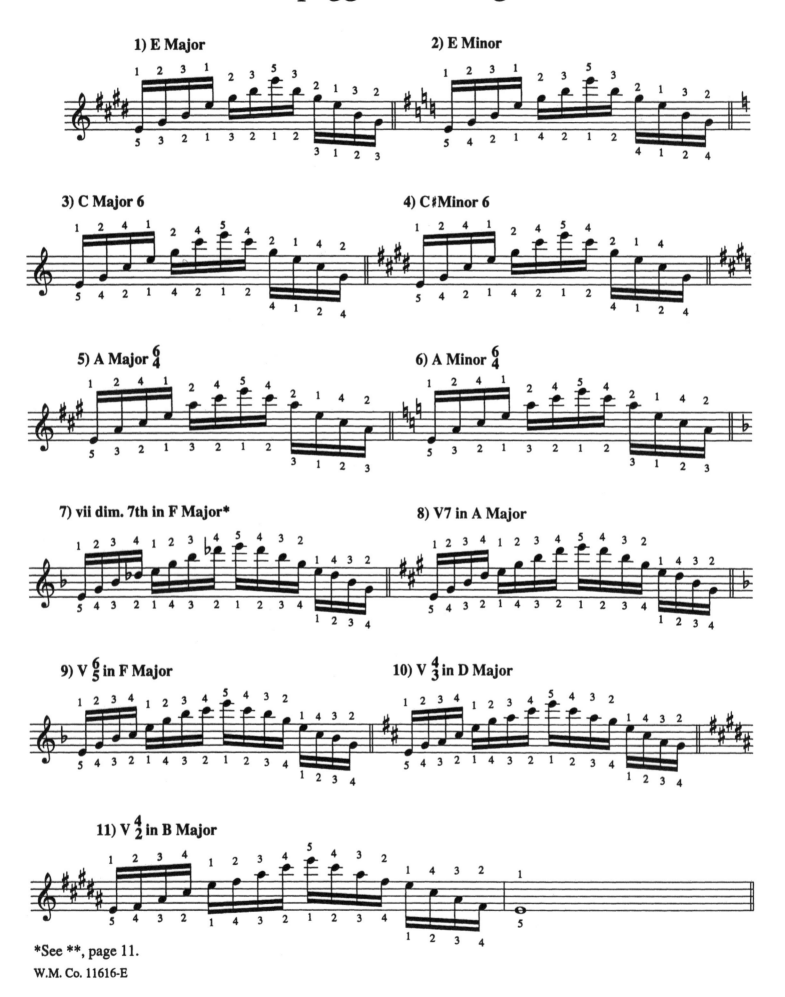

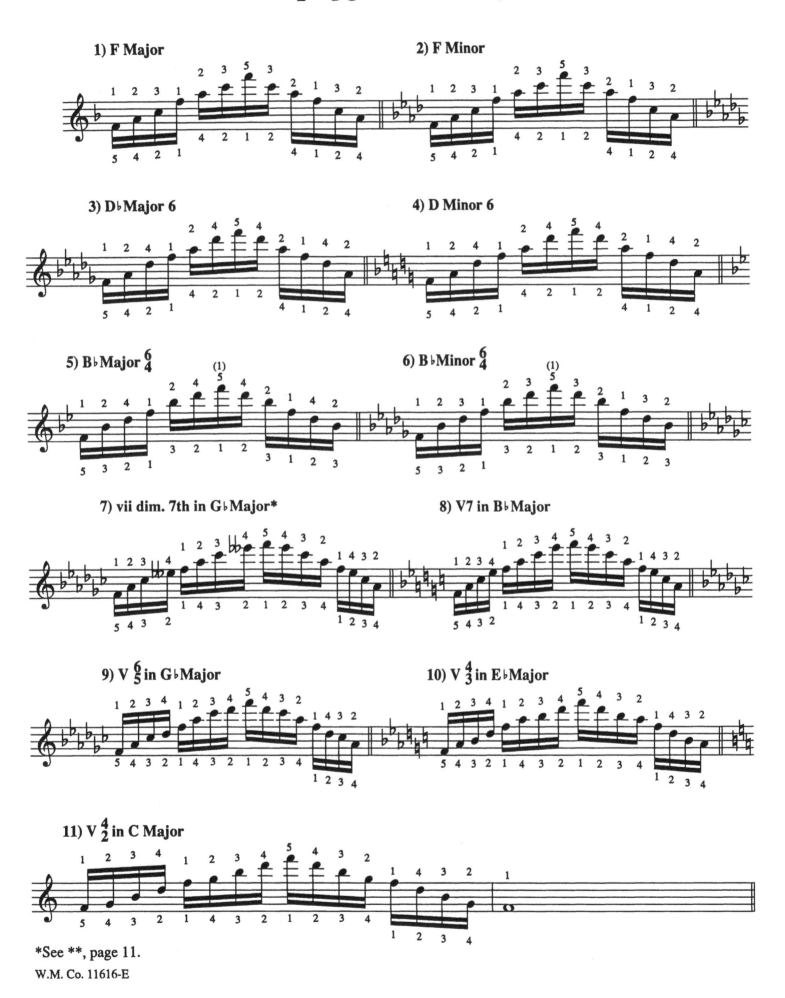

Eleven Arpeggios Starting from F

1) F Major

2) F Minor

3) D♭ Major 6

4) D Minor 6

5) B♭ Major $\frac{6}{4}$

6) B♭ Minor $\frac{6}{4}$

7) vii dim. 7th in G♭ Major*

8) V7 in B♭ Major

9) V $\frac{6}{5}$ in G♭ Major

10) V $\frac{4}{3}$ in E♭ Major

11) V $\frac{4}{2}$ in C Major

*See **, page 11.

W.M. Co. 11616-E

Eleven Arpeggios Starting from F♯/G♭

1) G♭ Major

2) F♯ Minor

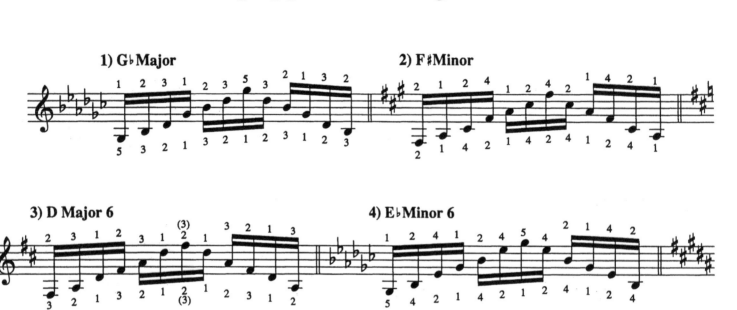

3) D Major 6

4) E♭ Minor 6

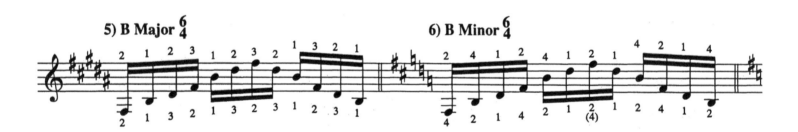

5) B Major $\frac{6}{4}$

6) B Minor $\frac{6}{4}$

7) vii dim. 7th in G Major*

8) V7 in B Major

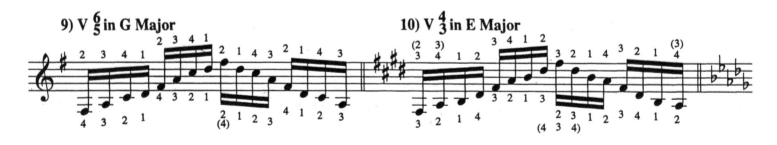

9) V $\frac{6}{5}$ in G Major

10) V $\frac{4}{3}$ in E Major

11) V $\frac{4}{2}$ in D♭ Major

*See **, page 11.
**Fingering for end of arpeggio.

Eleven Arpeggios Starting from G

1) G Major

2) G Minor

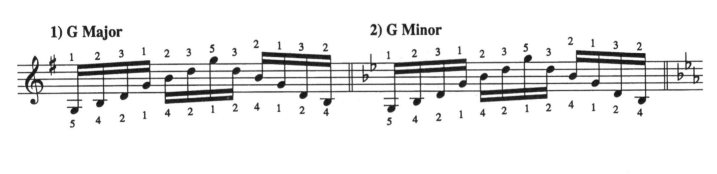

3) E♭ Major 6

4) E Minor 6

5) C Major $\frac{6}{4}$

6) C Minor $\frac{6}{4}$

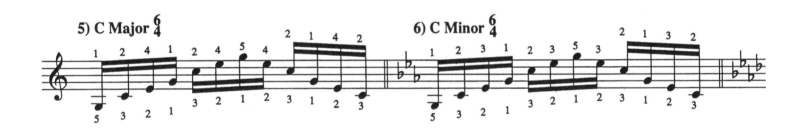

7) vii dim. 7th in A♭ Major*

8) V7 in C Major

9) V $\frac{6}{5}$ in A♭ Major

10) V $\frac{4}{3}$ in F Major

11) V $\frac{4}{2}$ in D Major

*See **, page 11.

W.M. Co. 11616-E

Eleven Arpeggios Starting from A♭/G♯

Eleven Arpeggios Starting from A

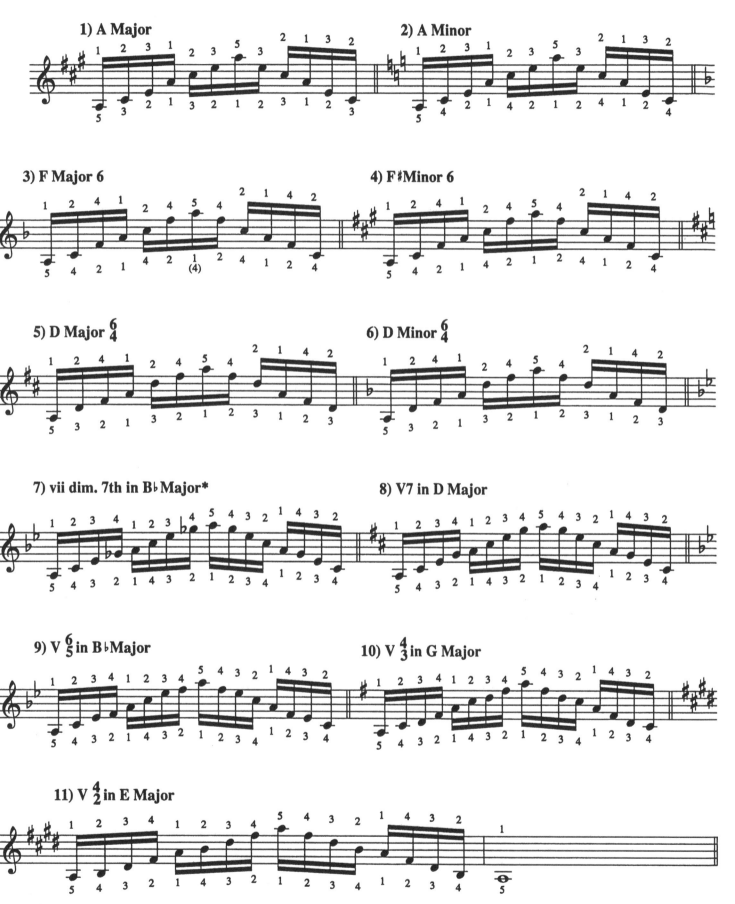

Eleven Arpeggios Starting from B♭/A♯

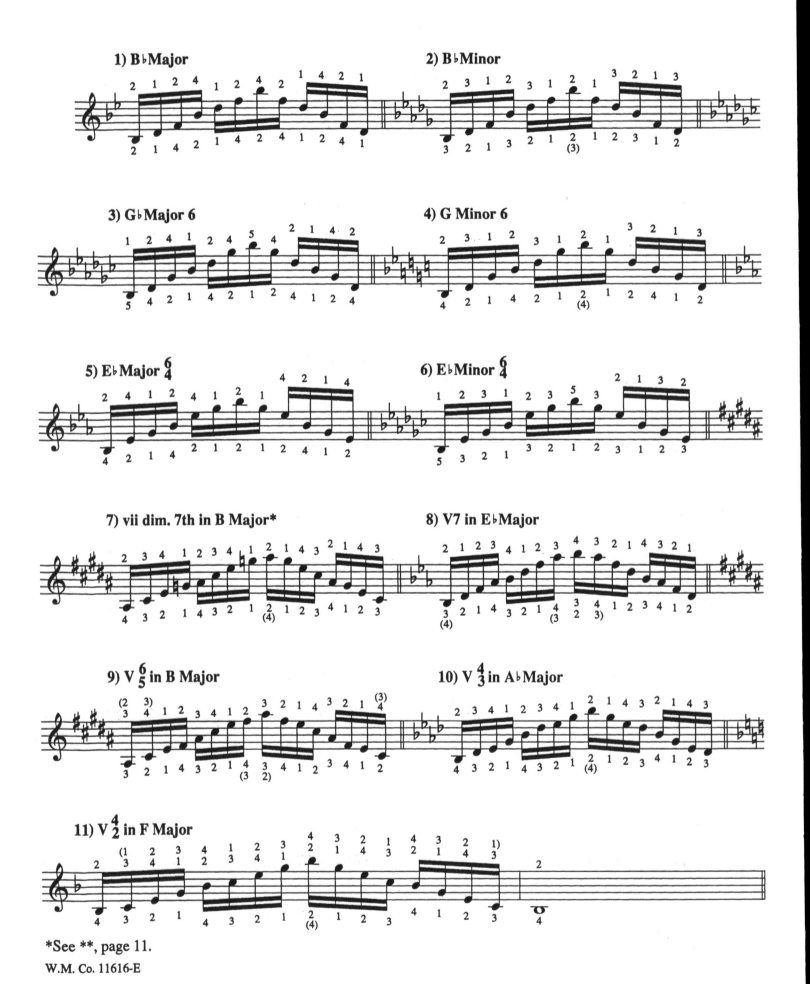

Eleven Arpeggios Starting from B

1) B Major

2) B Minor

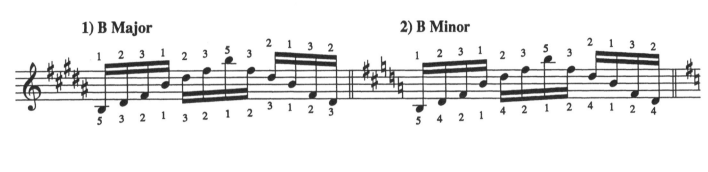

3) G Major 6

4) G♯ Minor 6

5) E Major $\frac{6}{4}$

6) E Minor $\frac{6}{4}$

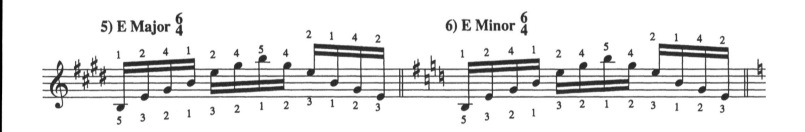

7) vii dim. 7th in C Major*

8) V7 in E Major

9) V $\frac{6}{5}$ in C Major

10) V $\frac{4}{3}$ in A Major

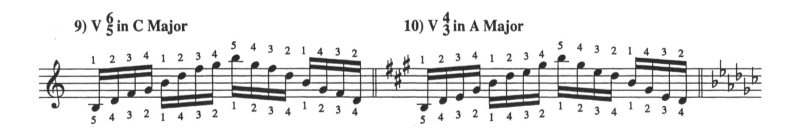

11) V $\frac{4}{2}$ in G♭ Major

*See **, page 11.

W.M. Co. 11616-E

Eleven Block Chords Starting from C*

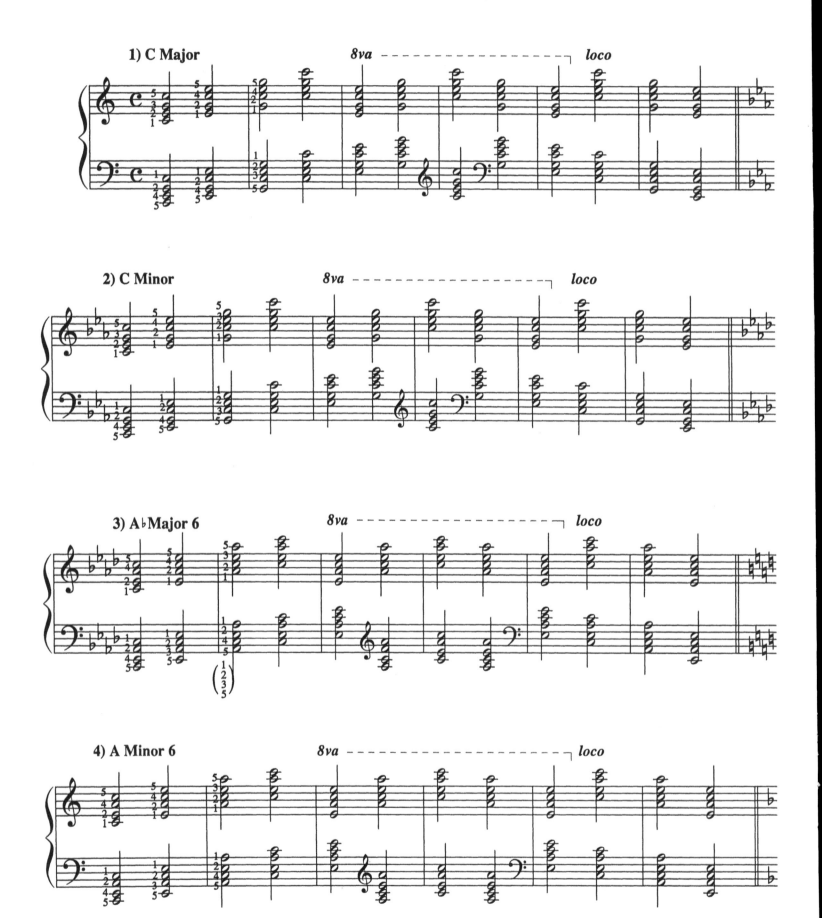

*Presented in Russian Harmonic Pattern; see *Introduction and Guide Book*, Part Three, Chapter XI.

W.M. Co. 11616-E

5) F Major $\frac{6}{4}$

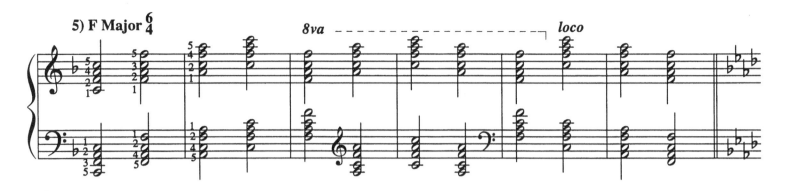

6) F Minor $\frac{6}{4}$

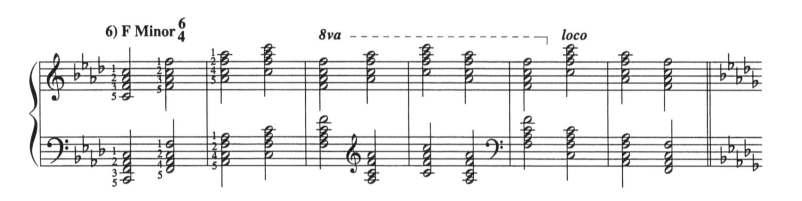

7) vii dim. 7th in D♭ Major

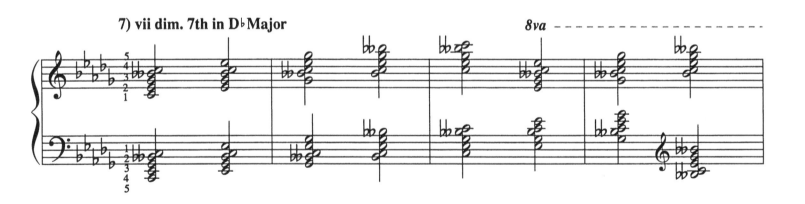

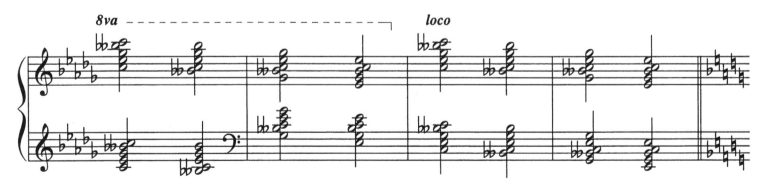

W.M. Co. 11616-E

8) V7 in F Major

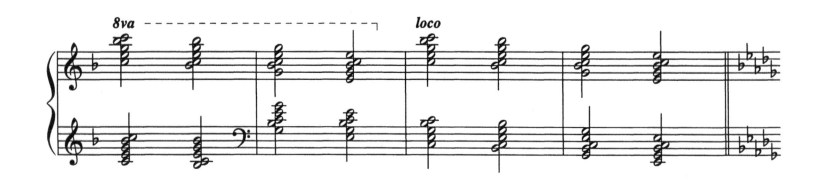

9) V $\frac{6}{5}$ in D♭ Major

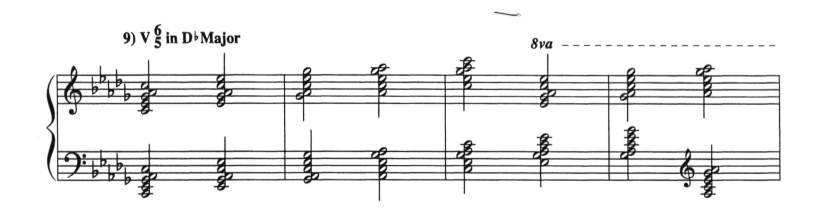

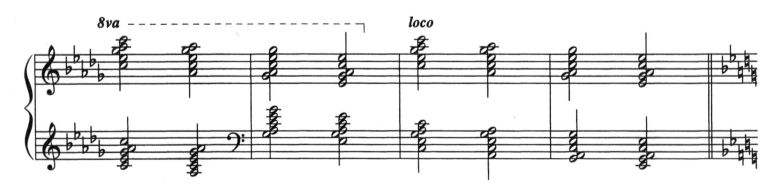

10) V $\frac{4}{3}$ in B♭Major

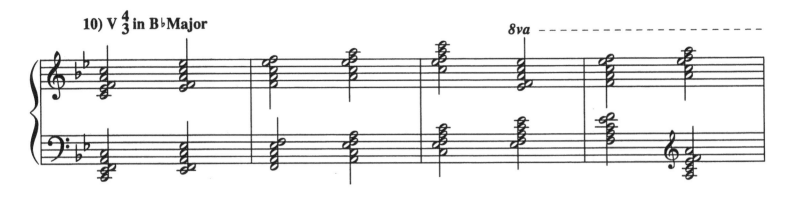

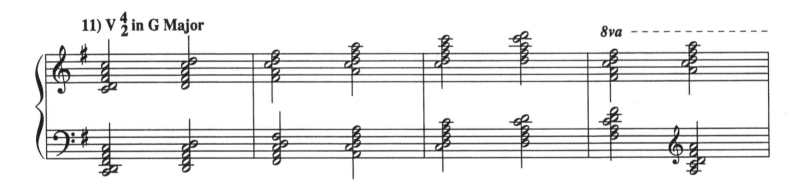

11) V $\frac{4}{2}$ in G Major

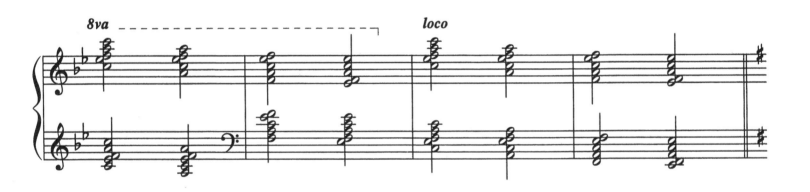

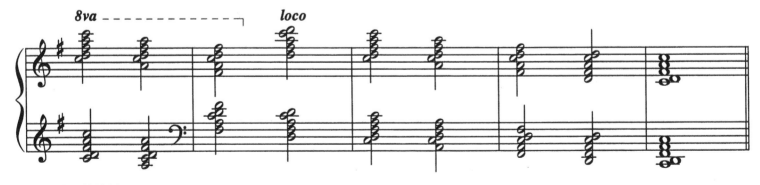

W.M. Co. 11616-E

Eleven Block Chords Starting from D♭/C♯

*See the seventh chords starting from C, pages 23-25. All the block chord exercises, starting from any note, should be played 2 octaves up and down.

W.M. Co. 11616-E

Eleven Block Chords Starting from D

1) D Major

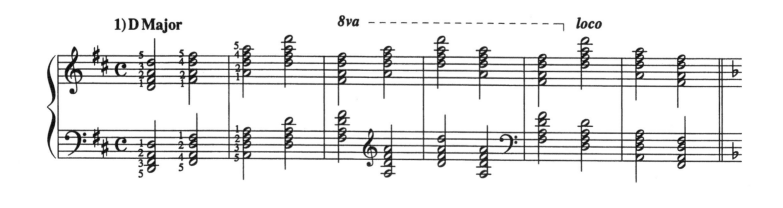

2) D Minor

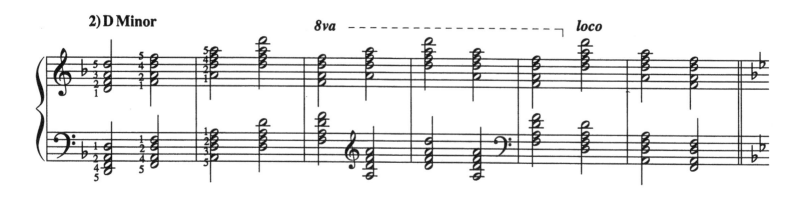

3) B♭ Major 6

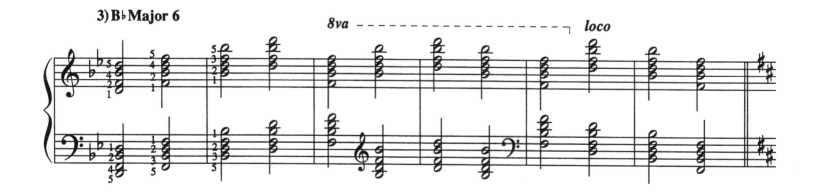

4) B Minor 6

W.M. Co. 11616-E

5) G Major $\frac{6}{4}$ *8va* - - - - - - - - - - - - - *loco*

6) G Minor $\frac{6}{4}$ *8va* - - - - - - - - - - - - - *loco*

7) vii dim. 7th in E♭ Major

(up and down two octaves)*

8) V7 in G Major   9) V $\frac{6}{5}$ in E♭ Major

(up and down two octaves)

10) V $\frac{4}{3}$ in C Major   11) V $\frac{4}{2}$ in A Major

*See *, page 27.
W.M. Co. 11616-E

Eleven Block Chords Starting from E♭/D♯

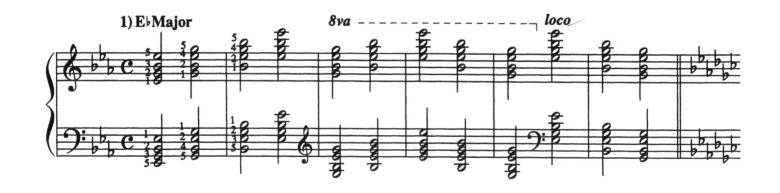

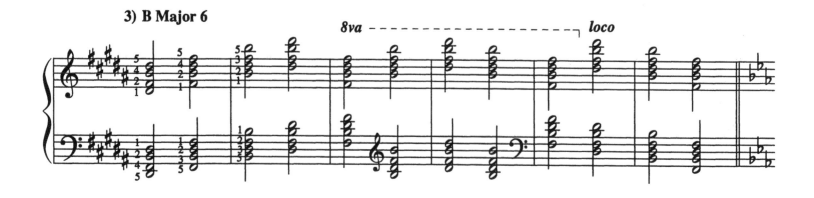

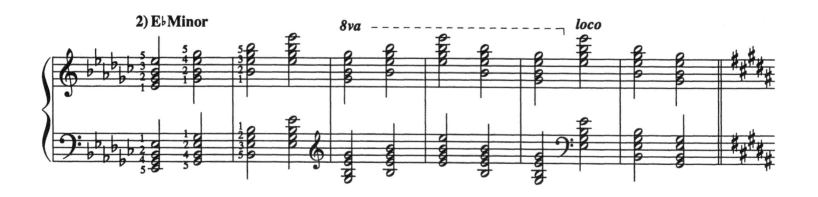

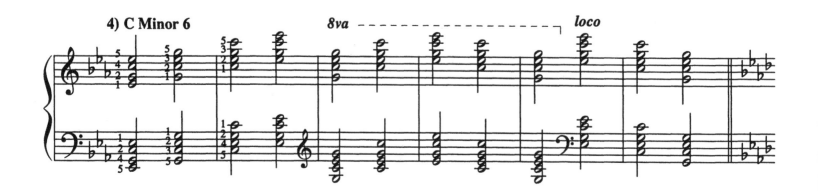

*See *, page 27.
W.M. Co. 11616-E

Eleven Block Chords Starting from E

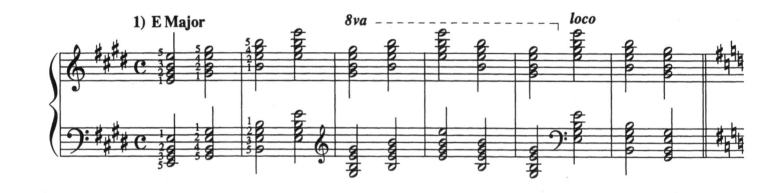

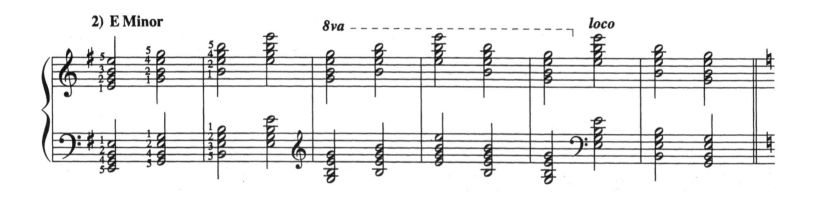

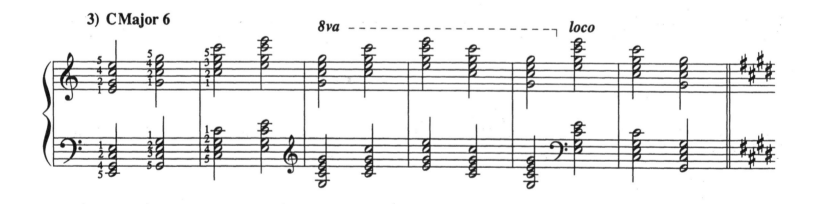

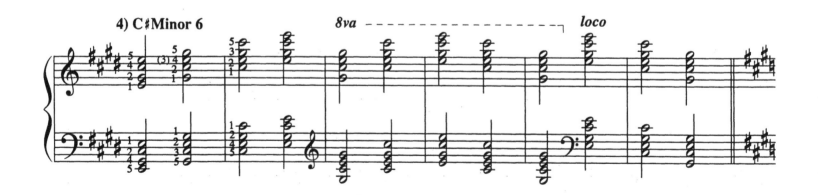

W.M. Co. 11616-E

Eleven Block Chords Starting from F

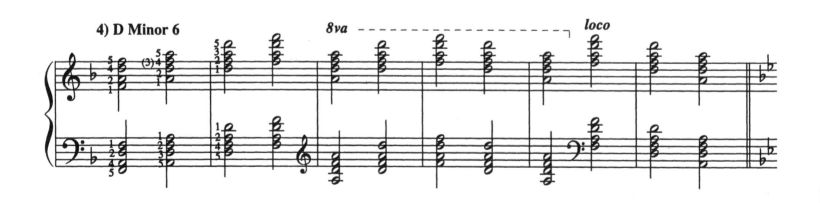

*See *, page 27.

Eleven Block Chords Starting from F♯/G♭

1) G♭ Major

8va – – – – – – – – – – – – – – – *loco*

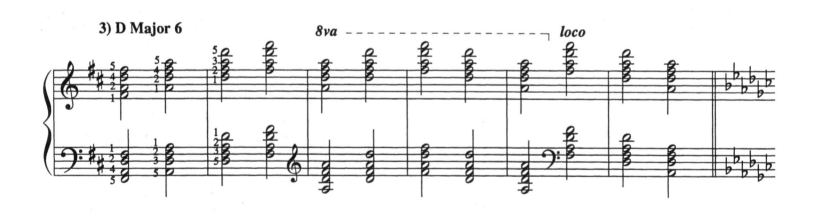

2) F♯ Minor

8va – – – – – – – – – – – – – – – *loco*

3) D Major 6

8va – – – – – – – – – – – – – – – *loco*

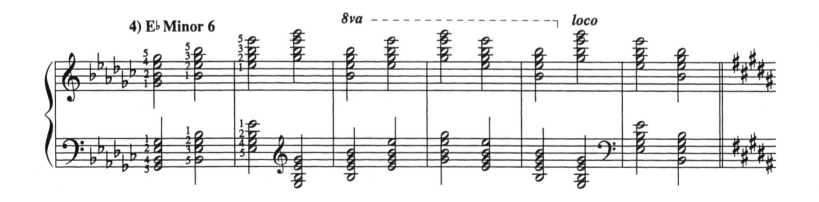

4) E♭ Minor 6

8va – – – – – – – – – – – – – – – *loco*

5) B Major 6/4

6) B Minor 6/4

7) vii dim. 7th in G Major*

8) V7 in B Major

9) V 6/5 in G Major

10) V 4/3 in E Major

11) V 4/2 in D♭ Major

*See *, page 27.
W.M. Co. 11616-E

Eleven Block Chords Starting from G

1) G Major

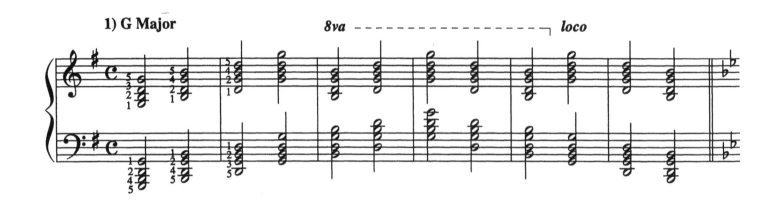

2) G Minor

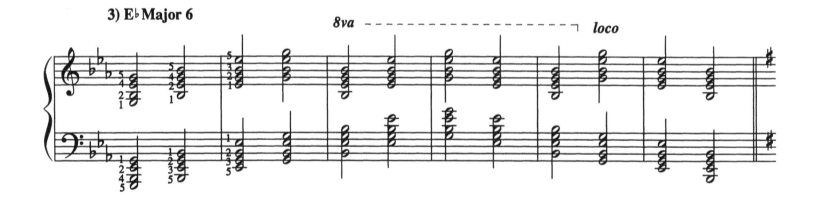

3) E♭ Major 6

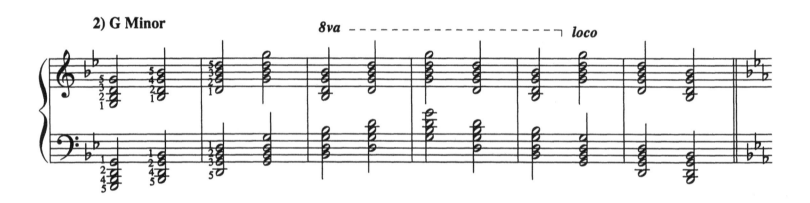

4) E Minor 6

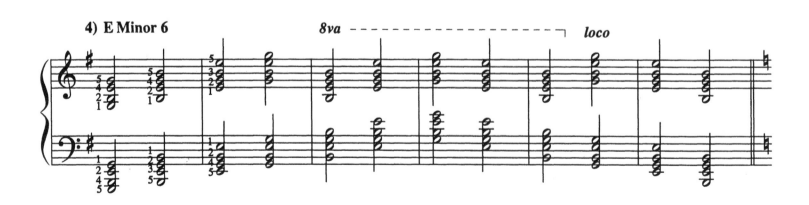

W.M. Co. 11616-E

5) C Major $\frac{6}{4}$

6) C Minor $\frac{6}{4}$

7) vii dim. 7th in A♭ Major*

8) V7 in C Major

9) V $\frac{6}{5}$ in A♭ Major

10) V $\frac{4}{3}$ in F Major

11) V $\frac{4}{2}$ in D Major

*See *, page 27.

W.M. Co. 11616-E

Eleven Block Chords Starting from A♭/G♯

5) D♭ Major 6/4

6) C♯ Minor 6/4

7) vii dim. 7th in A Major*

8) V7 in D♭ Major

9) V 6/5 in A Major

10) V 4/3 in G♭ Major

11) V 4/2 in E♭ Major

*See *, page 27.

W.M. Co. 11616-E

Eleven Block Chords Starting from A

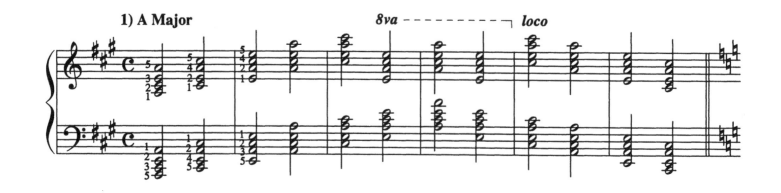

1) A Major

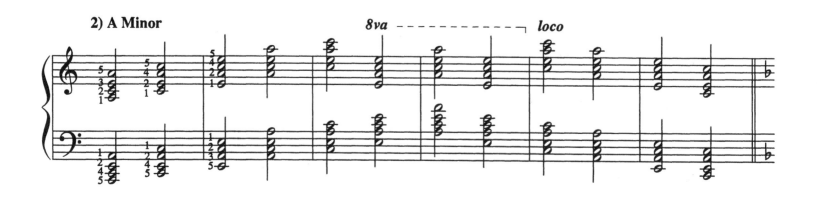

2) A Minor

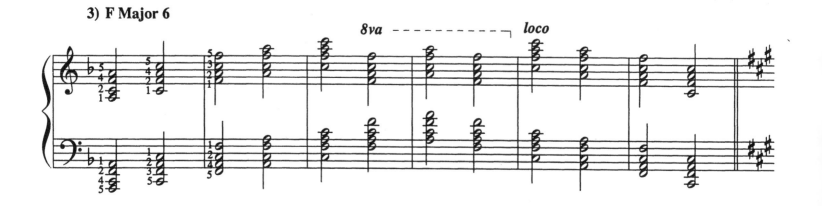

3) F Major 6

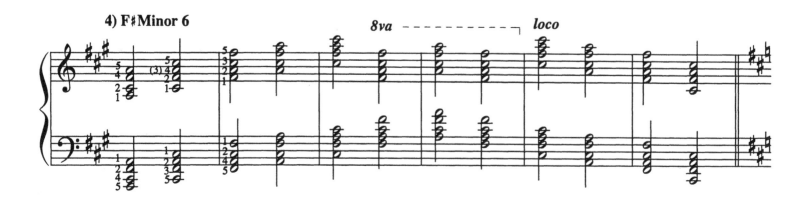

4) F♯ Minor 6

Eleven Block Chords Starting from B♭/A♯

1) B♭ Major

2) B♭ Minor

3) G♭ Major 6

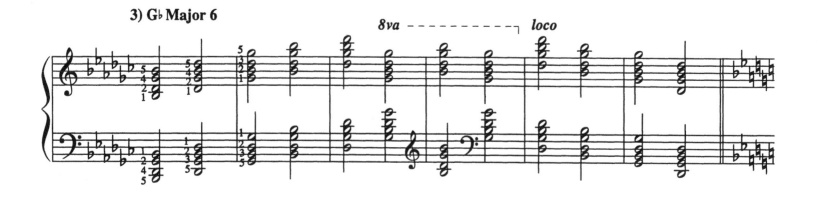

4) G Minor 6

W.M. Co. 11616-E

Eleven Block Chords Starting from B

1) B Major

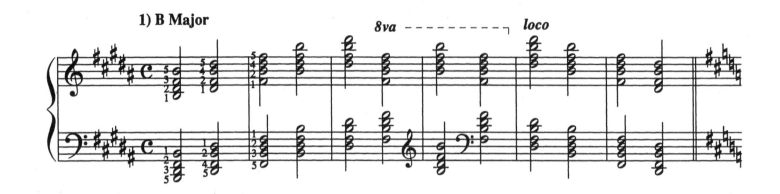

2) B Minor

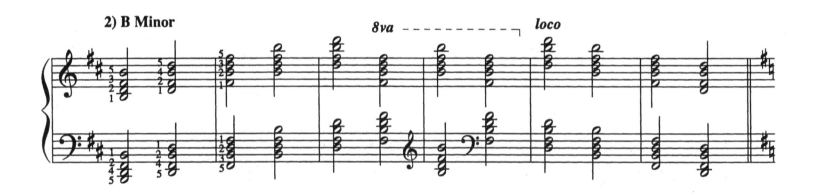

3) G Major 6

4) G# Minor 6

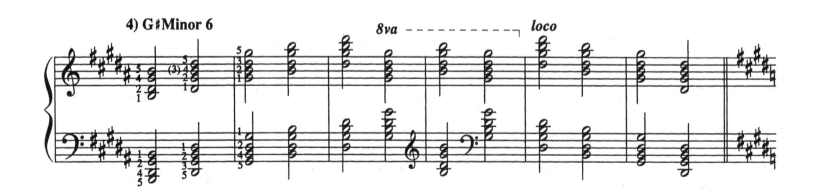

W.M. Co. 11616-E

5) E Major $\frac{6}{4}$

6) E Minor $\frac{6}{4}$

7) vii dim. 7th in C Major*

8) V7 in E Major

9) V $\frac{6}{5}$ in C Major

10) V $\frac{4}{3}$ in A Major

11) V $\frac{4}{2}$ in G♭ Major

*See *, page 27.

W.M. Co. 11616-E

Alexander Peskanov
On The Russian Technical Regimen

---Introduction & Guide ("Guide Book")

Complete instructions on how to practice the technical requirements of The Russian Technical Regimen

---Exercise Volume I, Scales in Single Notes

---Exercise Volume II, Broken Chords

---Exercise Volume III, Russian Broken Chords

---Exercise Volume IV, Arpeggios and Block Chords

---Exercise Volume V, Scales in Doubles Notes: thirds, sixths, and octaves

Instructional Videos, "In Search of Sound"

    Demostrations and performances by Alexander Peskanov

    (produced by Classical Video Concepts, Inc.)

---Piano Olympics Kit (Manual and Video)

An exciting Piano Event that helps teachers to engage students in practicing scales and exercises using the Russian Technical Regimen. Also, it offers the opportunity to demonstrate their accomplishments in the performance of their repertoire (Produced by Classical Video Concepts, Inc.)

---The Piano Video Exchange with Alek Peskanov

A revolutionary new way of communication between concert artist, student and artist/teacher. This personalized video program will allow the participants to make their own Video Presentation and receive a detailed critique from the artist presented by CVC Inc./Baldwin Piano and Organ Co.

---For further information contact:---
Classical Video Concepts, Inc.
P.O. Box 1930
West Babylon, New York 11704-1930
FAX (516) 669-1203

W.M. Co. 11616E